Managing a child with autism: A manual on how to interact with a youngster who has autism

LEAH J. ADAMS

Table of Contents

INTRODUCTION

(ASD) is a formative handicap brought about by contrasts in the mind. Individuals with ASD frequently dislike social correspondence and association, and limited or dull ways of behaving or interests. Individuals with ASD may likewise have various approaches to getting the hang of, moving, or focusing.

Being medically introverted doesn't mean you have an ailment or sickness. It implies your mind works another way from others.

It's something you're brought into the world with. Indications of chemical imbalance may be seen when you're extremely youthful, or not until you're more established.
Assuming you're mentally unbalanced, you're medically introverted for what seems like forever.
Chemical imbalance is not an ailment with medicines or a "fix". In any case, certain

individuals need backing to assist them with speclflc thlrıgs.

Being medically introverted doesn't need to stop you from having a decent life.
Like everybody, mentally unbalanced individuals have things they're great at as well as things they battle with.

Being medically introverted doesn't mean you can never make companions, have connections or find a new line of work. Yet, you could require additional assistance with these things.
Mental imbalance is a range. This implies everyone with mental imbalance is unique.
A few mentally unbalanced individuals need next to zero help. Others might require help from a parent or carer consistently.

A few medically introverted individuals have normal or better-than-expected insight.

A few mentally unbalanced individuals have a learning handicap. This implies they might find it hard to take care of themselves and need assistance with day-to-day existence.

Medically introverted individuals frequently have different circumstances, for example,

consideration shortfall hyperactivity jumble (ADHD)
dyslexia
nervousness
melancholy
epilepsy

We realize that there isn't one mental imbalance yet numerous subtypes, most impacted by a mix of hereditary and natural variables. Since chemical imbalance is a range problem, every individual with mental imbalance has an unmistakable arrangement of qualities and difficulties. The manners by which individuals with mental imbalance learn, think and issue tackle can

go from profoundly talented to seriously tested. Certain individuals with ASD might need huge help in their regular routines, while others might require less help and, now and again, live completely freely.
A few variables might impact the improvement of chemical imbalance, and it is much of the time joined by tangible responsive qualities and clinical issues, for example, gastrointestinal (GI) problems, seizures or rests issues, as well as psychological wellness difficulties, for example, uneasiness, sadness and consideration issues.

Indications of chemical imbalance generally show up by age 2 or 3. Some related advancement deferrals can show up significantly prior, and frequently, it tends to be analyzed as soon as a year and a half. Research shows that early mediation prompts positive results sometime down the road for individuals with mental imbalance.

CHAPTER 1

Signs of autism in children

As a parent or caregiver of an infant, you have an up-close view of your baby's development. You can see the small changes in day-to-day behaviors that indicate a baby is building new skills and abilities.

If you know what to look for, you may be able to detect early signs of developmental differences like autism. This is because the earliest signs of autism aren't the presence of unexpected behavior, but the absence of skill or ability that usually develops by a certain age.

The Centers for Disease Control and Prevention (CDC)Trusted Source reports that most parents with autistic children notice some signs within the first year, and

80 to 90 percent observe developmental differences by the time their child is 2 years old.

Your observations and instincts are important because identifying developmental differences early gives the child in your care the advantage of early diagnosis.

What are the signs of autism in babies?

Autism doesn't change a baby's physical appearance. The condition does affect how babies communicate and how they relate to the world around them.

Autism is described as a "spectrum" condition because signs, symptoms, and abilities can vary widely. If you notice any of these developmental differences, it's important to talk with your child's doctor or healthcare professional about them.

1. Declining eye contact

Babies typically make eye contact trusted
Source with other people from a very young
age. By 2 months, infants can typically
locate faces and make eye contact skillfully.
Eye contact later becomes a way of building
social relationships and gaining information
about their surroundings.

ResearchersTrusted Source has found that
babies who develop autism spectrum
disorder (ASD) begin making less eye
contact at around 2 monthsTrusted Source
of age. The decline in eye contact may be
an early indicator of autism.

2. Little pointing or gesturing

Babies usually learn to gesture before they
learn to talk. Gesturing is one of the earliest
forms of communication. Autistic children
generally point and gesture much-less
trusted Source than children with nonautistic

development. Less pointing can sometimes indicate the possibility of a language delay.

Another indicator of a developmental difference is when an infant's gaze doesn't follow you when you're pointing at something. This skill is sometimes called "joint attention." Joint attention is often decreased in autistic children.

3. Limited or no response to their name

At 6 monthsTrusted Source, most infants show an awareness of their names, especially when it's spoken by their mother.

Autistic infants show a developmental difference: By 9 months, many babies who later develop ASD don't orient to their names. ResearchersTrusted Source says this usually appears as a pattern of nonresponse, rather than a single instance.

4. Reduced emotion in facial
    expressions

Facial expressions are a nonverbal way to
communicate thoughts and feelings.

Research on emotional expression in
autistic infants is limited, but in
studiesTrusted Source involving school-age
children, researchers have found that
autistic children display less emotion
through facial expressions than children with
nonautistic development.

That doesn't necessarily mean autistic
children are feeling less emotion, just that
less of it shows on their faces when they do.

5. Delayed language or speech

Babies and toddlers start talking at different
ages.

ResearchTrusted Source shows that young autistic children often say and understand fewer words than children with nonautistic development at 12 months. If a child isn't saying single words by 16 months or isn't using two-word phrases by age 2, it's a good idea to talk with a pediatrician.

The National Institutes on Deafness and Other Communication DisordersTrusted Source say language development could be "uneven," with exceptional language development in some areas and impairment in other areas.

6. Regression

When an infant or toddler loses skills and abilities that had begun to develop, it can be an indication of autism. It can also be a profoundly difficult experience for parents and caregivers to witness.

Researchers don't know why regression happens. There are no known links to any childhood experiences, diseases, or medications.

As many as one-third trusted Source of autistic children lose skills after infancy and before preschool. Around 94 percent of the time, it's language skills that are lost. If your baby babbled, made eye contact, gestured, and displayed other social behaviors and stopped doing so as a toddler, it's something to discuss with your pediatrician.

Signs of autism in young children include:

not responding to their name
avoiding eye contact
not smiling when you smile at them
getting very upset if they do not like a
certain taste, smell, or sound
repetitive movements, such as flapping their
hands, flicking their fingers, or rocking their
body

not talking as much as other children
repeating the same phrases
Autism in older children

Signs of autism in older children include:

not seem to understand what others are
thinking or feeling
finding it hard to say how they feel
liking a strict daily routine and getting very
upset if it changes
having a very keen interest in certain
subjects or activities
getting very upset if you ask them to do
something
finding it hard to make friends or prefer to be
on their own
taking things very literally – for example,
they may not understand phrases like
"break a leg"
Autism in girls and boys

Autism can sometimes be different in girls
and boys.

For example, autistic girls may be quieter, may hide their feelings, and may appear to cope better with social situations.

This means autism can be harder to spot in girls.

CHAPTER 2

What Are the Causes of Autism?

Specialists don't completely see each of the reasons for mental imbalance range jumble. It is by all accounts hereditary, however things, for example, parental age and physician-recommended meds taken during pregnancy might be involved.

For example:

An individual is bound to be on the range if a sibling, sister, or parent is. However, it doesn't generally run in families.

Around 10% of children with ASD have a type of hereditary issue like Down disorder and delicate X condition. A huge Danish review tracked down a connection among ASD and high-level

parental period of one or the other parent.
Ladies recommended narcotics not long before pregnancy are likelier to have a kid with ASD.
A few kids who are on the range begin giving indications as youthful as a couple of months old. Others appear to have typical improvement for the initial not many months or long stretches of their lives and afterward, they begin showing side effects.

However, up to half of the guardians of kids with ASD saw issues when their youngster arrived at a year, and somewhere in the range of 80% and 90% saw issues by 2 years. Youngsters with ASD will have side effects all through their lives, however, it's feasible for them to get better as they progress in years.

The mental imbalance range is extremely wide. Certain individuals could have truly perceptible issues, while others could not. The consistent idea is contrasted in interactive abilities, correspondence, and conduct contrasted and individuals who aren't on the range.

A kid with ASD struggles with interfacing with others. Issues with interactive abilities are the absolute most normal signs. They should have cozy connections yet not know how.

Assuming your kid is on the range, they could show a few social side effects when they're 8 to 10 months old, including:

They don't answer their name by their most memorable birthday.
Playing, sharing, or chatting with others doesn't intrigue them.
They like to be distant from everyone else.

They stay away from or reject actual contact, including embracing.
They stay away from eye-to-eye connection.
At the point when they're disturbed, they could do without being supported.
They don't grasp feelings - - their own or others.
They may not loosen up their arms to be gotten or directed with strolling.

CHAPTER 3

7 Tips for Talking to Kids with Autism

Since one of the classic symptoms of autism is a marked deficit in verbal communication abilities, a common problem for applied behavior analysts and others who work with children and even adults with Autism Spectrum Disorder is simply being able to carry on a basic conversation. Something as simple as finding out what they want for lunch or whether or not they are happy or sad or indifferent about their current school assignment can be nearly impossible to find out if you rely on normal conversational methods.

But don't let that stop you!

There are ways to have conversations with autistic kids and you can make them easier by keeping the following tips in mind.

DO Make the Effort to Talk To Them

Because talking to kids with autism can be difficult, many adults take the easy way out and just avoid including them in conversations in the first place. But that's a mistake; both you and those children can benefit from attempts at conversation, even if they are not always successful.

There's also a tendency to assume that if an autistic child doesn't respond or shuts you down that they don't like you or don't want to talk. But that's not always the case; that signal would be clear from a neurotypical individual but for someone with ASD, it's just a part of the syndrome. Don't take it personally, and don't stop trying to gently involve autistic kids in your conversations.

They probably want to engage, they just have more difficulty figuring out how.

Pick Your Moments

Not just any time is the right time to talk to an autistic child. Many of them have very particular schedules and rhythms to their behavior. If you interrupt them when they are deeply involved in something else, you're not likely to get through and engage them as you had hoped to.

Similarly, it's often not a good time to engage when the child is already wound up about something. Excessive stimuli can cause children with ASD to shut down. Wait for a calm and quiet moment if you want to have a conversation.

Talk About What They Want To Talk About

One approach that will never get you far with an autistic kid is to try to force the

conversation in a direction you want it to go.
At best you'll get ignored; at worst, they'll
shut down or have an outburst.

Obsessions are part of the syndrome and
an obsession means a lot of discussion
about one particular thing. You might find it
boring or simple but you'll find far more
engagement by sticking to the topic that the
child wants to discuss.

Keep It To the Point
Stay away from allusions, metaphors, or
abstract statements. Autistic kids generally
will not be able to interpret any kind of
communication that relies on reading your
internal emotional state or any kind of
subtext.

Keep your sentences short and direct.

The pace of the conversation needs to be at
a level the child can maintain. For most of
us, processing sentences as we hear them

is second nature and happens almost instantly. Autistic kids have to work to parse out what they hear, however. Give them the time they need to do it.

If Speaking Doesn't Work, Try Writing!
If you get to sticking points in the conversation, try restating what you just said on paper. Draw a picture or write the words down and show them. ASD patients tend to think visually, so even if they don't immediately understand what they just heard, they might get the same message if you put it on paper so they can see it.

Pay Attention To Non-Verbal Signals

Because autistic kids can have a lot of trouble manipulating language as well as understanding it, they often develop various types of behaviors that signal things that you might expect them to verbalize. Certain motions or actions they use while speaking might tell you more than the words they say if you pay attention and learn to interpret them.

Remember They Are Just Kids!

Autistic kids may not act a lot like neurotypical children but remember you're still talking to someone whose thoughts and attitudes are being formed in an immature brain.

With a little practice, you may find that you can talk to autistic kids just as easily as any kid. The results, for both you and the child, can be both positive in terms of their development of communication skills and enjoyable as you make an interpersonal connection.